Janyeid K. Castro Sousa
Jemmla Trindade
Elias N. Costa

# Teaching Science in Grajaú

Janyeid K. Castro Sousa
Jemmla Trindade
Elias N. Costa

# Teaching Science in Grajaú

## Analysis of the assessment tools used by elementary school teachers in the urban area of Grajaú-MA

ScienciaScripts

Cover image: www.ingimage.com

This book is a translation from the original published under ISBN 978-3-330-75631-1.

Publisher:
Sciencia Scripts
is a trademark of
Dodo Books Indian Ocean Ltd. and OmniScriptum S.R.L publishing group

120 High Road, East Finchley, London, N2 9ED, United Kingdom
Str. Armeneasca 28/1, office 1, Chisinau MD-2012, Republic of Moldova, Europe
Printed at: see last page
**ISBN: 978-620-8-27693-5**

## SUMMARY

# 1 INTRODUCTION

In order to carry out the work of a teacher, it is necessary to plan the activities that involve: the choice of teaching method, didactic procedures and the evaluation process. Among these, we can cite the assessment process as the most complex of all the actions in the teaching-learning process, in any form of education.

Recognizing learning assessment as a continuous process is not common, as it is often expressed as the numerical result of one-off tests, which often do not express the students' real learning.

It is part of the teacher's job to check and judge the performance of the students, evaluating the results of the teaching. To do this, the teacher needs to have various evaluation techniques and instruments that can diagnose the beginning, middle and end of each stage of teaching. Assessment is always present in the classroom and is part of the school routine, so it is the teacher's responsibility to perfect their techniques.

Working with subjects that make up the Exact Sciences is no longer an easy task, given the great difficulty students have in constructing knowledge in these subjects, just as it is no easy task to assess students coherently in these subjects that require a great deal of dedication from the students.

Considering both the complexity and the importance of this subject, the aim of this work is to gain technical knowledge about the history of school assessment in Brazil, the main assessment instruments, which are the most used by teachers in the Brazilian education system and the importance of formative assessment for chemistry teachers.

Based on the whole context surrounding the evaluation of teaching processes in general, this work proposes a brief reflection on the evaluation of learning and the processes adopted by teachers who teach Chemistry in public primary schools in the urban area of the city of Grajaù, state of Maranhão. The work, which is based on the teachers' conceptions, was aimed at analyzing the data provided by the teachers working in the schools through fieldwork, with the intention of identifying the pedagogical performance in the use of evaluation instruments for Chemistry classes in schools in the city of Grajaù - MA.

This work also aims to provide the author with better academic and professional training, through a qualitative study with a review of literature already published by authors who deal with the issue of student evaluations, in order to make pedagogical activity increasingly dynamic and productive in the education and social formation of students in public schools in the Brazilian education system.

## 2 PEDAGOGICAL ACTION AND ITS EVALUATION INSTRUMENTS

For a chemistry teacher to begin their work in a classroom, they need to have not only an academic degree in chemistry, but they also need to learn assessment techniques and know how to use the many assessment resources correctly in their educational activities aimed at the teaching and learning process.

"It is clear that tests and exams are important instruments in the evaluation process, but it is important to know whether these results will be seen in an evaluative or examining way." (LUCKESI. 2003, p. 11.).

All pedagogical work is related to what has already been developed in terms of teaching techniques based on the principles of pedagogy as a science of formal education techniques. As happens in schools with primary school chemistry teachers in the city of Grajaù - MA, the assessment instruments are mastered through higher education and the practice of the teaching professional.

Teaching itself is an action that has been transformed into a profession by the need to use teaching methods that are constantly evolving and, likewise, assessment instruments have also multiplied throughout the existence of the Brazilian education system. The techniques used to use these instruments have been modernized to meet the different challenges of the educational process.

An elementary school teacher must know how to use assessment instruments to improve his or her teaching practice, seeing the teaching and learning process as continuous and subject to improvement.

## 2.1 History of school evaluation in Brazil

School assessment is an extremely important didactic resource for formal teaching activities in Brazilian schools. It has been used since the first rural schools, run by Jesuit priests, in which they educated Indians, black slaves and poor bastards. Its history is intertwined with pedagogy itself, as there is no teaching-learning process without assessment.

Luckesi (2003, p. 11) comments: "Historically we have come to call the practice of monitoring the assessment of student learning "school learning assessment", but in fact we continue to practice "exams".

Throughout history, school evaluation in Brazil has been a challenge for educators, pedagogues and school management who, through the Pedagogical Political Project (PPP), seek to adjust the realities of each school unit's limited resources when it comes to planning the application of evaluation tools to the educational practice of primary school students. Since the earliest schools, in which assessments were merely "exams" of written and oral tests, according to the criteria of the educators (Jesuit priests or not), assessment instruments have modernized as theoretical and practical tools throughout the history of Brazilian education.

Ramos (2002) states that the school is still an important and necessary social space in our culture. This is the reason for the permanent reconstructive movement to make this space evolve, in order to meet the social demands of this and new times. (RAMOS, 2002 p. 25). Therefore, it is within schools that pedagogy and its many assessment mechanisms have been developing and modernizing throughout Brazilian education to meet the needs of the teaching and learning process for both educators and students in curricular subjects such as chemistry.

## 2.2 Evaluation as a tool in the teaching and learning process

In order to deal with the issue of school evaluation, it is first necessary to understand its characteristics and its importance for the formal teaching-learning process.

In the pedagogical world, it is known that in order for the teacher to measure the level of learning of the students, it is necessary to have proof of the learning results, and it is based on this principle that the students are subjected to periodic evaluations that enable the educator to assess their performance with their teaching method and the learning and training capacity of the students.

The Houaiss Dictionary of the Portuguese Language (2001, p. 353) defines the term evaluation as: "[...] the verification that aims to determine the competence, progress, etc. of a professional, student, etc." On the other hand, evaluation itself has a logical meaning, a purpose of making it possible to be sure that something is right or wrong, thus helping the teacher's activity (SANT'ANNA, 1995).

As the work of teaching and training students unfolds during the school year, teachers need to be aware of their attitude as educators, whether their performance is satisfactory, and the most direct way of assessing this is through tests and quizzes, checking in the students' grades whether or not there is support for their efficient performance.

Teaching involves the teacher as a whole; their practice is the result of knowing, doing and, above all, being, meaning a commitment to themselves, to the student, to knowledge and to society and its transformation (GRILO, 2002, p. 78).

The assessment factor within an elementary school classroom for students studying chemistry, for example, involves a responsibility to measure the social, cultural, ethical and global formation of the students. All of this is part of the pedagogical practice of every school in the Brazilian education system (SANT'ANNA 1995).

That's why when an education professional, for example, proposes a change in the evaluation process, these changes must be studied politically by the school's coordinators, within the parameters of efficiency and the fulfillment of the school's social function. In this way, political and cultural parameters function not only as a way of promoting efficiency in the learning of curricular content, but also the overall education of students.

"It is necessary to investigate the real purpose of evaluation, so that we can define it, seeking to understand and deepen what it involves in order to effect changes in pedagogical practices." (CORSETTI, *et al*, 2001, p. 76).

A good teacher always sees assessment mechanisms as more than just an opportunity to check how well his or her students are learning, but also as an opportunity to assess himself or herself as an educator, capable of modernizing himself or herself through ongoing training.

Aware that the educational needs and the cultural and social training of their students is something that is evolving and that increasingly requires the modernization of pedagogical practices in order to meet the social, historical, political and even technological demands of a globalized world, it becomes coherent for teachers to always be open to the knowledge of new evaluation practices.

Assessment mechanisms must be developed, mastered by educators and used by them in accordance with the reality of schools, seeking to transform education into a training tool for the job market, for socializing students and preparing them for the challenges of a modern and competitive world (SOUSA, 2014). In other words, the act of evaluating is much more for the teacher and other employees in the administration of a school unit than seeking to achieve certainty about the students' learning, in relation to what they are taught by the curricular subjects of their course, but rather a way of measuring the efficiency of the school's activities in its responsibility to prepare students for life.

In practice, this requires pedagogical skills on the part of the teacher when it comes to promoting the informal assessment of their primary school pupils in the form of questions relating to the ideology of some of the content presented, the philosophy of education seeking, in this case, to awaken logical and coherent thinking.

Villas Boas (2006, p. 23) confirms:

> Informal assessment gives teachers a great deal of flexibility in their judgment and should be practiced responsibly. An example of this is the customary "rounding of grades", which consists of the teacher increasing them according to criteria that he or she defines and which are not always made explicit. This rounding is done on the basis of this form of assessment.

Finally, it doesn't matter whether informal or formal assessment is used by teachers in primary education, it is always an instrument of approval or disapproval of what is presented by the students when they are tested, an instrument of self-assessment by educators and students, of educational policy and of the fulfillment of the school's socio-cultural function.

## 2.3 Written production as a tool for assessment in chemistry

If a teacher's evaluation is oral, it doesn't require writing, but, on the contrary, the most common evaluation process in schools throughout Brazil is written tests (in chemistry, for example), the teacher's conference expressed by written notes (SANTOS, *et al*, 2009).

Writing is always part of any school learning process. It is the basis of the work of the teacher, who writes on the board, and the students, who write in their notebooks. When fieldwork is given, the teacher writes down what it is about and then the students do their research and wait for their grades. From there, the assessment is (usually) done by the teacher in writing.

In order for the teaching and learning process to be possible in the teacher/student educational interaction, reading and writing are indispensably necessary and, following this line of reasoning, the fact that written production has historically been an assessment tool in the form of tests, quizzes and various exams for the formal educational institution is justified.

Writing to learn means discovering relationships between ideas, selecting and ordering ideas and data, or even giving form to experiences we have been through so that we can understand them more clearly (BERNARDO, 2000, p. 54). The simple act of a teacher correcting a test by marking the correct answers with a pen and the wrong ones with a mark reflects this.

Among the most commonly used assessment tools at primary school level in chemistry lessons, for example, written production is in first place. It is the most widely used method of assessment, as it is the simplest and the most direct and practical when it comes to checking students' learning in the form of grades.

> It starts from a set of assumptions regarding the reading of the texts we examine. The materials analyzed constitute a set of signifiers. The researcher attributes meanings to them based on their knowledge and theories. The emergence and communication of these new meanings is the aim of the analysis (MORAES, 2003, p. 5).

Writing as an assessment tool is a great responsibility for the teacher who analyzes the answers given in tests and quizzes taken by the students, simply because it excludes the mathematical resource at the time of the conference.

The educator's logical/coherent thinking therefore needs to be judged by different parameters, such as: the ability to distinguish coherent and cohesive texts, the analysis of the student's philosophical thinking and the justification of what the question requires of the answer in any written test or quiz.

The production of writing as an evaluation tool is also a question of evaluating the didactics applied to the teaching and learning process by the teacher, i.e. the reading and writing used in the teaching/learning process should be evaluated for their efficiency in the classroom.

Bernardo adds (2000, p. 53):

> Reading to learn and writing to learn. The preposition para identifies the aim, the purpose that we emphasize so much and the leap that we want to make. We are therefore talking about reading and writing as a means of learning, including from themselves. The content (be it mathematics, history, chemistry, physics or even Portuguese) that you want to develop may seem to take precedence over reading and writing, but you can't give them up as instruments to support learning.

Every piece of writing therefore has a basis for supporting its reality as an assessment tool. Whether it's through an understanding of the evaluation of pedagogical activity, which uses reading and writing for formal teaching, or through an understanding of the students' written responses in their exams or tests to be critically evaluated by the teacher in charge.

Writing as an assessment tool follows a natural historical order in the Brazilian education system, as we only know of public schools, for example, where writing is a routine part of teaching and learning. That's why written assessment is the most widely used, because it's the most direct and requires the least training for teachers who, in most cases, only have to assess students' tests using a textbook.

It is necessary to write, and from this the quality of the texts evolves and the confidence and confidence in one's own productions also grows (MORAES, 2003, p. 2). Now, if writing is part of the learning process with interpretative readings that increase students' intelligence, writing could only be the basis of the main assessment tool for school teachers in the Brazilian education system.

## 2.4 Evaluation methods

Understanding the forms of modern pedagogical evaluation, by their specific technical criteria, such as: criterial, diagnostic and regulatory, is a way of systematizing the understanding of school evaluation in all its fullness.

There are many ways of assessing students' learning outcomes. And all forms of school assessment have been developed and put into practice due to their recognized importance, the efficiency that justifies the effort to learn them by the Pedagogy student.

The meaning of evaluation is by means of an instrument of evaluation by selection, accuracy of production in which, by defining grades, students can be classified as: good, regular, excellent or even insufficient.

Luckesi (2003, p. 35), states:

> This kind of attitude means that the act of evaluation doesn't serve as a pause to think about the practice and return to it, but rather as a means of judging it and making it stratified. "[...] with its classificatory function, assessment does nothing to help progress and growth. Only with a diagnostic function can it serve this purpose."

In general, the different forms of assessment are applied because of the acceptance of their importance, their efficiency in assessing both student learning by checking grades and the quality of teaching, according to the results of the teaching methods applied by the educator.

In the case of qualitative assessment, where the teacher needs to interpret texts produced by the students as answers to test questions, for example, this requires thinking skills, coherence and the appropriation of interpretative means acquired through teaching experience can help in making precise decisions of right or wrong, or partially right, in the performance of the teacher who assesses by their logical-interpretative criteria.

Moraes (2003, p. 3), confirms: "Doing qualitative analysis of materials implies assuming interpretations of the statements of discourses, from which the texts are produced, being aware that this always involves one's own subjectivity."

All the forms of assessment that a teacher can use in the course of his or her work must have a defined purpose and be part of the teaching method that uses assessment processes as a didactic resource to improve learning and teaching. There are many ways of assessing work and the techniques used must always follow criteria that are learned during the academic course.

### 2.4.1 Criterion evaluation

As the name implies, criterial assessment prioritizes specific criteria, for example, if the chemistry teacher teaches something about environmental conservation, the students must produce essays that are faithful to the proposed learning theme.

This form of assessment is preceded by guidance on what is to be learned (in specific), so that learning has a certain learning criterion.

### 2.4.2 Diagnostic assessment

In the case of the diagnostic assessment model, the focus of the analysis should be on the students' learning performance by evaluating the results of tests, for example. This involves a description of the strengths and weaknesses of the students' ability to learn.

Diagnostic evaluation is also used to measure the efficiency of the teacher's work, either through self-assessment or by a pedagogical board qualified to make changes to teaching methods, according to a technical analysis.

According to Santos (2009):

Diagnostic assessment involves describing, classifying and determining the value of aspects of behavior. Diagnostic practice seeks to verify the presence and absence of acquired knowledge, as well as learning conditions that act as prerequisites for the student to start learning at a certain level. However, this type of action does not necessarily involve the teacher intervening to make possible improvements.

In the case of diagnostic assessment, this is the most dependent on self-evaluation and teacher/student/parent interactions in order to diagnose the origin of any problem that hampers good performance at school by realities outside the school in the search for a solution.

### 2.4.3 Regulatory evaluation

This form of assessment is complementary to formative assessment, i.e. it seeks to promote teaching methods capable of overcoming the difficulties identified in the teaching and learning process in order to optimize student learning.

## 2.5 Formative assessment to improve learning Chemistry

Pedagogy in itself is a way of teaching with formalities, mediating knowledge and the student promoting knowledge in a systematized way with formal teaching didactics.

Hoffmann adds (2009, p. 41):

> The essence of the formative conception lies in the teacher's involvement with the students and their awareness of their commitment to the students' learning progress. The formative vision is based on the assumption that without guidance from someone who is mature enough to do so and without adequate cognitive challenges, it is unlikely that the student will acquire the knowledge necessary for their development in the most meaningful way possible. The teacher's mediating role is essential in formative assessment.

In this reality of (formative) evaluation, the student cannot evaluate himself or herself, the active presence of the teacher with his or her pedagogical skills that come from the ability to teach with formalized teaching is essential.

Thus, it is through the presence of the teacher, with their academic training, mastery of teaching methods and assessment that technical assessment becomes possible for the teacher with professionalism.

He points out (LOCH, 2000, p. 34) about formative evaluation:

> It is always led by the teacher; it is designed to promote learning; it takes into account personal progress, the effort put into it and other aspects not made explicit in the curriculum, i.e. it is not entirely based on criteria; in formative assessment, ideas that could be classified as "mistakes" here provide diagnostic information aimed at reorientation; students play a central role and must take an active part in their own learning.

With formative assessment, the teacher is able to have greater control over the teaching and learning process of chemistry students in primary school, with the educational process working within pedagogical criteria in their formal teaching.

### 2.5.2 The self-assessment of chemistry students in basic education

When chemistry teachers teach in primary schools, they use participatory teaching methods, the basic characteristic of which is teacher/student interaction in philosophical, reflective and critical dialogues about the content taught, its importance and what the students think about any controversial topic. Stimulating critical opinion is the basis of the participatory method.

When teachers manage to stimulate their students' critical sense, they become more committed to knowledge, identify their own characteristics as learners and accept the importance of evaluating themselves as thinking, critical beings who are committed to their own education. "When assessing their students, teachers are assessing themselves, although most are not aware of this or admit it." (GATTI, 2003).

In other words, evaluation in itself is a learning tool for both educators and educators in relation to students' activities, and even for students who need to be constantly taught to evaluate themselves in order to overcome cognitive deficiencies and overcome any limitations in teaching resources, for example, which is common at primary school level in public schools.

"Students should feel motivated to look for ways of constructing knowledge, just as their teacher does. This means that the creative teacher induces the student to create as well". (DEMO, 2002, p. 22).

Through the exercise of pedagogy, the teacher must stimulate the students

to understand their responsibility to improve every day as a student, that evaluation is always a way of seeking excellence through discipline. And that this applies both to those who educate and to those who position themselves as student-students, in other words, there is a difference between students and pupils.

In any primary school classroom, for example, the assessment process is in itself a pedagogical mechanism whose main purpose is to assist the teaching and learning process. And students must know how to position themselves as learners, accepting their autonomous characteristics in the midst of this formal educational process.

Costa (2003, p. 57) reminds us:

> (...) Autonomy is the faculty to govern oneself; the right or faculty to be governed by one's own laws; emancipation; independence. It is undoubtedly a complex and very controversial subject when discussed. At present, many still see autonomy as a process of individualism, in which the subject develops in search of emancipation. However, this conquest leads to an extreme that is not desired by all, the path of selfishness and centralization of information, of coming and going without taking account of one's motives, of living according to one's fantasies and inclinations. In this sense, the individual seeks independence, but isolates himself from the group, uses the knowledge he has acquired for his own benefit, only passing on information when he can somehow gain an advantage.

That's why chemistry students in basic education need to be instructed by their teacher on how to manage the most efficient forms of self-assessment, on how important this can be for them to improve their learning performance both in self-assessment in the classroom and in out-of-class studies. And, the educator must master techniques for classifying student evaluations.

> (...) mistakes are considered constructive. The teacher's concern is to intervene so that the student can move on to more developed learning. Both the student's learning and the teacher's intervention are in a constant process of evaluation with the aim of moving forward and not just classifying (ABRAHÂO, 2000, p. 41).

Whenever, in the midst of a teaching and learning process, a teacher (of chemistry, for example) identifies some weakness in his didactic posture or in his mastery of social relationships with his students, or even the ethical posture of his students, he is seeking to improve the quality of his service.

In the case of the assessment of chemistry students, for example, it is still necessary to make assessments of the students' ability to self-evaluate, guiding the best ways of doing this as a means of reinforcing their efforts in the art of transmitting knowledge and forming critical, ethical students with the capacity for self-learning.

### 2.5.3 Evaluation in theoretical and practical classes of the subject Chemistry

Assuming that a school has a scientific research laboratory for chemistry lessons, educators need to master techniques for evaluating both their theoretical and practical teaching activities.

In the case of the evaluation of theoretical teaching with explanatory and expository lessons, the teacher evaluates the grade that the student achieves in order to identify the strengths that should continue to be stimulated and the weaknesses to be combated. And the assessments themselves are changeable according to the different interests of the teachers. "Changing assessment probably means changing the school". (ENRICONE AND GRILO, 2002, p. 127).

If there are traditional forms of assessment in the classroom (grades for tests, quizzes and out-of-class assignments, for example), on the other hand, the forms of assessment in the case of activities in the chemistry laboratory, in practical scientific research, require interpretation of what is created scientifically by the student.

In these cases, a chemistry project developed should be evaluated for its efficiency by the chemistry teacher, its dynamism and whether the artifact was made according to the teacher's guidelines. In other words, this is the case with the practical assessment model.

The evaluation process in elementary schools that have a chemistry laboratory is complementary, i.e. the teacher gives his lessons in the classroom and evaluates the students' theoretical learning, but when they are taken to the research laboratory, in the same way as the practical lessons, the evaluations are also based on practical production.

Teaching and assessing theoretical lessons prepares students for teaching and assessing practical lessons in the laboratory. The lectures and reviews with assessments in the classroom must come first, and then the laboratory.

# 3 METHODOLOGY

The starting point for this work was a bibliographical survey on the central theme, which extended from the beginning to the final draft of the work. The search for theoretical references is of great importance when writing scientific papers, as it provides a basis for knowledge about what has been researched (PIZZANI *et al*, 2012). According to Boccato (2006, p. 266) a bibliographical search should provide learning about a particular area of knowledge; it should facilitate the identification and selection of methods and techniques to be used by the researcher and provide subsidies for writing the introduction and review of the literature and writing the discussion of the scientific work.

In the second phase, the aim was to observe the facts and have informal conversations with professionals who work in education, in order to obtain more information about the assessment instruments and, in the third phase of the research, the aim was to collect data that would not have been possible through bibliographical research and observation alone. To do this, we used interviews as a research tool, which is one of the techniques most used by researchers to collect data.

According to Rosa and Arnoldi (2006 p.17 apud FERES E FERES JÙNOR 2011), the interview is one of the data collection techniques considered to be a rational form of conduct by the researcher, previously established, to efficiently direct a systematic content of knowledge, in the most complete way possible, with the minimum effort of time.

The type of interview used was semi-structured, guided by a script of questions, which allows for flexible organization and broadening of the questions as the information is provided by the interviewee (BELLEI et al, 2008) and which, according to FUJISAWA (2000), is one of the most widely used models. After the interview, the data collected from the teachers was analyzed.

The results of the practical research with chemistry teachers in schools offering basic education in the city of Grajaù - MA, were approached using technical research procedures using a descriptive approach, describing the characteristics of those interviewed.

Reaffirms Figueiredo (2008, p. 203):

> It has a descriptive-exploratory approach, characterized as one that is responsible for describing the characteristics of a given population or phenomenon in order to make it more explicit, whose technical procedures will be bibliographic research and data collection.

To collect data in the field, five primary schools were selected, coded as Schools E1, E2, E3, E4 and E5, all located in the urban area of the city. These schools were chosen on the basis that they have the largest number of pupils of any primary school in the city. In total, 15 (fifteen) teachers were interviewed who were either trained in the subject (Chemistry) or had been hired to teach the subject in that area. The interviews sought to collect data on assessment, its characteristics, how it is applied and its importance for the development of the teaching and learning process. The interviews were conducted from November 5 to 30, 2015.

In order to organize the work, the data obtained will be presented in the form of dissertated information and also in the form of statistical data presented by illustrative graphs. In the case of subjective answers (written and not marked), the interviewees will be represented by the letter "P", which stands for teacher.

# 4 RESULTS AND DISCUSSION

One of the biggest challenges for any teaching professional is the assessment of student learning, from its preparation to its judgment. It is perhaps one of the stages of the teaching-learning process that requires the most attention due to its importance in this process. Considering the importance of this stage, the interviewees were asked what they understood by assessment in the teaching-learning process.

According to the teacher (P2): "Assessment is basically checking the content learned". For another interviewee, (P13) "Assessment is a way of measuring students' learning of certain content covered in class." Other interviewees gave very similar answers: "It's a necessary method for measuring knowledge in the teaching-learning process" (P7); "It's a mediating process where we observe whether the students have achieved the knowledge developed by the teacher" (P10).

It can be seen from the answers mentioned above that the teachers' conceptions are similar on some points, especially when it comes to the simplistic concept of assessment as a (quantitative) measure of knowledge.

In purely quantitative assessment, the concern is with quantity, with grades, with the aim of classifying the student's learning after the application of some assessment instrument. According to Santos, *et al* (2001), in this form of assessment, the student performs and the teacher judges, i.e. the student rarely participates and self-assessment is disregarded. Therefore, this type of assessment alone does not make it possible to analyze the student's learning process, which path he or she took to reach the result that was awarded a grade.

Although some teachers focus on assessment only in quantitative terms, others see it as a way of checking their teaching methodology and even the interaction between teacher and student: "Assessment is a way of checking whether your methodology is being effective" (P6); "It's a support for the teacher to find out whether their teaching methods have achieved their objectives during the teaching/learning process." (P 11); "It's a way of exchanging knowledge with the student" (P6). (P 11); "It's the exchange of knowledge between the student and the teacher". (P 15); "Very good in that it brings the teacher closer to his students and they interact better." (P 9).

Traditional assessment has been synonymous with measurement. It has been restricted to observing student performance, forgetting that educational processes involve not only the students, but also the teachers and all the interaction between them and the context in which the educational process takes place. Rarely do teachers take into account the reflection of their teaching practices in the evaluation process. However, evaluation, as a means of verifying the effectiveness of the teaching methodology, is a way for teachers to assess and improve their teaching procedures (SOUSA, 2010), in which case it takes on a guiding role for the teacher.

The interaction between teacher and student is extremely important in this process, as it involves both parties. Sant'anna (1995, p.27) states that "assessment will only be efficient and effective if it takes place in an interactive way between teacher and student, both moving in the same direction, in search of the same objectives".

According to Gipps (1998, p. 65 apud SOUZA E MENEZES, 2014, p.166), a change of concept is underway in the area of assessment, moving from a model of tests and exams that values the measurement of quantities of knowledge learned, to a model in which learners will have the opportunity to demonstrate the knowledge they have built, how they have built it, what they understand and what they can do, in other words, a model that values quantitative and qualitative learning during the learning process itself.

Some teachers presented their vision of evaluation, considering not only the quantitative aspect, but also the qualitative: "Evaluation consists of verifying student learning, both qualitatively and quantitatively" (P1) "Analysis of educational practice and effective student learning". (P 5). "Assessment is observing the student from their behavior, work in class and activities for home, their participation in class, answering questions and finally the test for the teacher to see if the students have assimilated the content." (P 8); "It's an instrument that contributes to the construction of knowledge and plays a fundamental role in helping to develop learning (P7); "Differentiated methods of assessment with an emphasis on the real situation of the students and the means that most facilitate the observation of knowledge for them". (P 12).

The term assessment refers not only to the quantitative aspects of learning, but also to the qualitative aspects, covering both the acquisition of knowledge and information resulting from the curriculum content, as well as students' skills, interests, attitudes and study habits (SOUSA, 2010). In learning assessment, the teacher's observations should not allow the results of periodic tests, which are generally of a classificatory nature, to be overvalued to the detriment of their daily observations, which are of a diagnostic nature.

The interviewees mentioned above (P1, P5, P7, P8 and P12), show in their answers that they have a broader view of the importance of assessment for their activities as chemistry teachers, while they present their answers in accordance with their aspirations as primary school educators, but the important thing, as Oliveira and Moraes (2005, p.17) point out, is that there should always be a discussion (reflection) of the objectives you want to achieve and the proposed assessment instruments.

"Studies have already shown the need for teachers to have opportunities to continually discuss the objectives and assessment instruments they are using, in order to take ownership of these new resources and, in fact, be helped to reorganize their teaching tasks when using them." (Oliveira and Moraes 2005)

The type of assessment method was investigated with the interviewees. With regard to assessment practices, the question was asked as to which modality is generally adopted by teachers. The answers are shown in Figure 1.

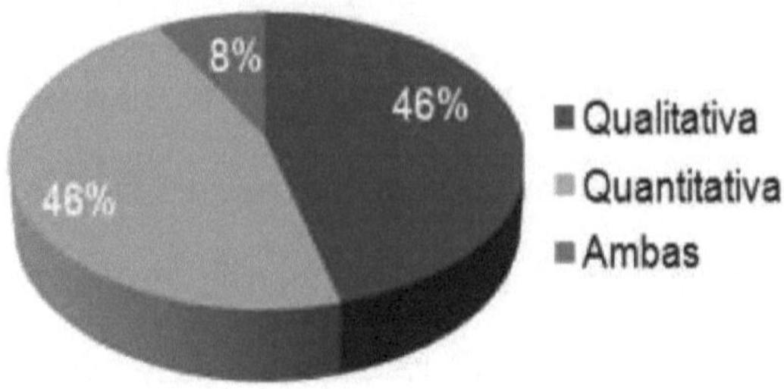


**Figure 1:** Types of assessment practices applied by chemistry teachers at the schools surveyed in Grajaú-MA.

Of the teachers interviewed, 46% (corresponding to seven teachers) said they used qualitative assessment, while another 46% said they used quantitative assessment. Only 8% of those interviewed said that they apply both types of assessment.

Understanding that the two modalities, in isolation, do not represent a complete evaluation, because **quantitative evaluation** is seen only as a measure and is therefore misused, and qualitative evaluation is lost in the subjectivity of teachers and students, it would be interesting for teachers to adopt both modalities when evaluating learning. It is suggested that for this type of question there may have been a lack of knowledge of what each type of assessment is really about, but as this difference was not addressed in the questionnaire, this statement should not be made.

Still in the context of assessment methods, teachers were asked whether assessment is done using concepts or whether it is done by assigning grades. Figure 2 shows the results of this question.

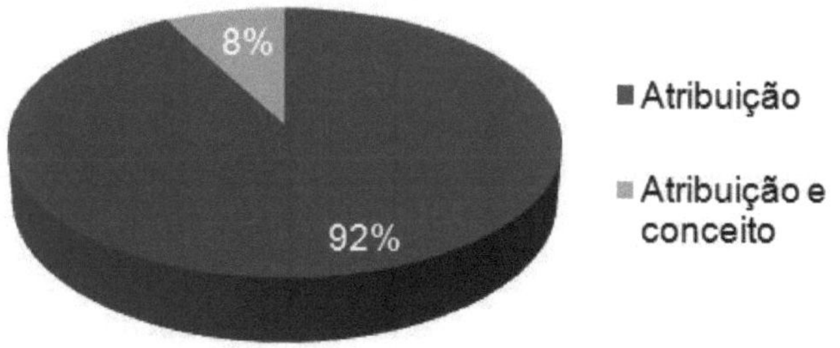


**Figura 2:** Form of assessment by the teacher

Figure 2 shows that almost all of the interviewees use the grading method. This result was to be expected considering that Maranhao state primary schools standardize grades as the final result of a learning process. Only 8% chose the alternative of assigning a concept.

The results of this question once again lead us to reflect on the degree of knowledge that teachers have about what qualitative assessment is, since it is usually done by assigning concepts, accompanied by an opinion. Considering that 46% of them said they used qualitative assessment, it would be coherent if a proportional number of teachers worked with concepts.

Sâ (2013) states that the attribution of concepts, accompanied by a report, are good resources, as they make the student's abilities clear, as well as "breaking the rigidity of grades". However, a brief analysis of the situation in public schools, in particular, leads to the conclusion that it would not be feasible to give an opinion on each student's development, with the aim of assigning concepts, considering the high number of students each teacher works with.

As a result, the teacher would have to spend an enormous amount of time on this type of assessment procedure.

In order to assess learning at school, various formal instruments can be used, such as: written tests, oral tests, seminars, debates, among others. In this respect, the teachers indicated some of the instruments (or strategies) they use most to assess students in the subject of Chemistry.

Of the fifteen (15) teachers interviewed, fourteen (14) cited the written test as their most used assessment tool. Lists of exercises were mentioned by thirteen (13) of them. Seminars were also mentioned by seven (7) of the interviewees. Other instruments such as group work (2 teachers), individual work (1 teacher), experiments (2 teachers), bibliographical research (1 teacher) and gymkhana (1 teacher) appeared in the interviewees' answers.

According to the teachers, most of them use written tests as an assessment tool. Objective tests are very useful in assessment, as long as they are well formulated and have clear objectives (ALVARENGA, 1999). It is extremely inappropriate to complicate the wording of the question in order to get in the way of the student and, likewise, it is inappropriate for the teacher to turn the test into a time to punish the student. In addition, the teachers themselves must prepare the tests and quizzes for their classes, taking into account what was actually taught and how it was taught. Thus, copying tests that have already been given is not an appropriate procedure for assessing the learning of a particular group (ALVARENGA, 1999).

As has been said, the test is one of the applied instruments that can be useful for assessing learning, and it is dependent on how it is formulated. In this context, teachers were asked what they consider important when preparing an assessment.

The overall responses of the 15 teachers interviewed to this question were as follows: - Content studied - (cited by 8 teachers) - Degree of difficulty - (cited by 2 teachers)

- Relationship between theory and everyday life (contextualized): (cited by 3 teachers).

Other answers were mentioned only once: Make the questions clear and objective; Level of the students; Consistency with the objectives; Exam questions; Interaction in the classroom.

The data on what is considered most important when it comes to preparing an assessment was quite consistent with the reality experienced by Chemistry teachers in Grajau's schools, since in many statements it is clear that the teacher's understanding of assessment is related to a test. But it is important to remember that a test is not an assessment, it is just an instrument used to verify learning. Assessment is a more global, continuous process.

According to several researchers in the field of education (CORSETTI, 2001; SANTOS, 2009; SOUSA 2010), the main concern when preparing an assessment should be to fulfill the objectives defined in the planning.

For assessment to be coherent, it needs to be understood as a continuous process. In order to get to know the teachers' conceptions in this respect, they were asked whether assessment is carried out specifically at pre-established times, such as bimonthly assessments. Only 27% answered yes (Figure 3).

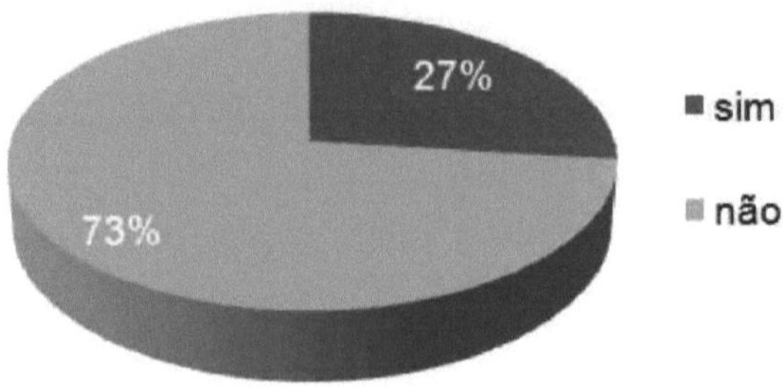


**Figura 3:** Evaluation done at pre-established times

Figure 3 shows that the majority of chemistry teachers (73%) answered that they don't carry out assessments at pre-established times, which means that most teachers carry out various assessments without a strict prior program.

The small proportion (27%) who only take assessments according to the pre-programmed schedule of bimonthly exams (one-off assessments) should at least rethink this practice, because this kind of attitude ends up guiding the actions of teachers and students, making the aim of teaching be to prepare students to do well in the exams. As a result, students will only study for the assessments. In this sense, assessment is not characterized as a continuous process.

Chemistry is one of the subjects that make up the Exact Sciences, along with Physics and Mathematics. Subjects in this area generally tend to have low scores in assessments across the board. We therefore asked the teachers what they thought were the most influential factors in low performance in chemistry.

This question, which is open-ended, has a certain subjectivity if we realize that the possibilities for answers are very wide-ranging, for example, the school history (preparation in previous grades) and the financial difficulties of students in basic education in public schools can, in themselves, give rise to a range of possible answers. However, some information was identical from the fifteen (15) interviewees, namely:

- Lack of student interest: (cited by 5 teachers)
- School-based problems (reading, calculations): (cited by 5 teachers)
- Lack of school structure: (cited by 5 teachers)
- Unqualified teachers: (cited by 2 teachers)
- Interpretation and understanding of the questions: (cited by 2 teachers)

Other answers were mentioned only once: student and teacher demotivation; lack of understanding of the content; few professionals; teacher methodology; level of abstraction; number of students per class; number of subjects. The interviewees also responded verbally that the parents of many students are not very interested in their children's schooling, that there is a history of poor textual interpretation skills due to poor financial conditions and low investment in basic public school education.

The factors listed by the interviewees corroborate those cited by various researchers in the country's schools. The work carried out by Silva (2010), in which he looked at students' difficulties in Chemistry and Physics at a school in Goiânia, cites the lack of contextualization and, consequently, students' lack of interest, as factors that influence low performance in these subjects. He states that "students don't show the necessary commitment, as they are unable to satisfactorily relate some of the content worked on in the classroom to their everyday lives, which ends up causing them to lose interest in the subject as a whole". Other works, such as Carvalho's (2007) and Jesus and da Silva's (2012), state that students lack some of the fundamentals of mathematics and criticize the ways in which exact subjects are taught, which do not value abstraction.

Poor student performance often gives the impression that this result depends solely on the student, for which the teacher has no responsibility (COLLARES; MOISÉS, 1994), but it is worth remembering that learning is a collective process that must have the effective participation of both students and teachers.

In cases where the majority of the class performs poorly in the assessments, the teacher is expected to take some differentiated action. Teachers were asked if they do this and, if so, what these actions are (Figure 4).

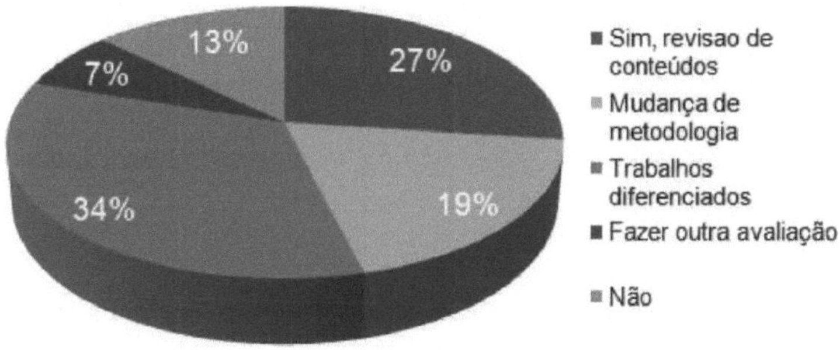


**Figure 4:** Differentiated action for cases of low student performance

According to Figure 4, 13% of the teachers (equivalent to 2 teachers) said that they do not take any kind of differentiated action. The rest said that they take a variety of actions. Of the group who said they take differentiated action, 34% (5 of the 15 interviewees) said that they do differentiated work; a further 27% (4 teachers) said that they deal with students' poor performance by reviewing content already covered in class. Changing the methodology is an attitude taken by 19% of those interviewed and, finally, only 7% choose to do another assessment.

It is considered that the feedback from the verification of student learning, through different assessment instruments, is important for the development of student performance. Taking this factor into account, it was verified whether teachers usually give feedback to students on the results of the assessments.

Everyone answered yes to this question:

"Yes, revision". (P 1); "Always". (P 2); "Yes, periodically an analysis is carried out and displayed individually". (P 3); "Things happen normally, I'd never manage it if the whole teaching staff didn't take part". (P 4); "Yes, as mentioned,

I hand them in, correct them, answer questions, show the class average, the % of students with grades above 7.0 and compare them with the previous two months and other classes, ask for suggestions for improvement and explain the results." (P 5).

Yes, it's important to do this, because in this way we can reduce learning deficiencies". (P 6); "Sometimes, when the result wasn't as expected and it's necessary to have a chat to find out what was missing and even revise the content" (P 7); "Yes, I always answer the assessments to show where they went wrong" (P 8); "Yes, for a better result and to take advantage of the moment when everyone is present". (P 9); "Yes, I talk about the subject given and what is likely to be in the test". (P 10); "Yes, the students need feedback, it's necessary to discuss with the students the answers that weren't understood (correct)." (P 11); "Yes, we always correct and I show them where it was wrong and the right way to do it." (P 12); "Yes, I make comments on the questions and clarify some doubts." (P 13); "Yes". (P 14); "It's always good to remind students of their real situations. But it's not always a good idea to keep putting pressure on students about bad grades." (P 15).

In the interviews with these teachers, the results point to a conformity of pedagogical procedures aimed at feedback in relation to the results of the evaluations.

It is therefore understood that all the interviewees are aware that this feedback is important, as it is understood that correcting tests or any other assessment tool is nothing more than reading the assessment data. Therefore, in addition to awarding marks, the teacher needs to use the results obtained by the students to identify the aspects that have not been well assimilated, which will allow them to return to these aspects to reinforce learning in order to improve low performance. In addition, poor results can be well managed pedagogically by the teacher so that they become an opportunity to correct mistakes. In this context, errors are seen as a clue that indicates how the student is relating the knowledge they already have to the new knowledge they are acquiring (a process of construction and reconstruction). Errors, in this case, no longer represent the absence of adequate knowledge and become a new starting point.

Therefore, evaluation only makes sense, as has already been said, if its results allow both students and teachers to reflect on the pedagogical processes developed.

## 5 FINAL CONSIDERATIONS

In view of all that has been said in this work, which portrays the assessment procedures of teachers who teach chemistry in the urban area of the city of Grajaù, it can be said that many teachers have a misconception of learning assessment. It was observed that there is a lack of understanding of assessment as a process and not just as one-off events.

The process of evaluation is certainly not simple, as it requires, above all, reflection on this action. It is therefore understood that a professional who is qualified to enter a classroom and work as a teacher needs to be constantly improving their teaching techniques, as is the case with assessment instruments. Continuously reflecting on the many techniques and modalities that must be applied in order to achieve different assessment purposes, both in terms of the competence of the teaching methods used and the students' ability to learn.

It is understood that the forms of assessment of students' academic performance have been focused mainly on the awarding of grades. Another form, less used by teachers, but which is very important, is written production as an assessment tool. This form is known as subjective responses, which require the teacher to be able to interpret what the students have done.

I believe that the objectives focused on learning assessment, its form, modality, instruments, among others, were achieved. The topic addressed in this work was of great importance, since it provided a reflection for those interviewed on the subject and also for the author of this work. I learned from both forms of research, qualitative and quantitative, and I believe that they will be useful to me in my work as a teacher and in the creation of future educational projects.

# REFERENCES

ABRAHĂO, M, E, M, B, et al. *Avaliaçâo e erro construtivo libertador:* uma teoriapràtica includente em educaçâo: Porto Alegre: EDIPUCRS, 2000.

ALVARENGA, Georfravia Montoza. A Commitment to Teaching and Learning. Nùcleo de Estudos e Pesquisa em Avaliaçâo Educacional, 170 p. Londrina, PR, 1999. Available at: http://www.moodle.ufba.br/mod/book/view.php?id=14311&chapterid=10893. Accessed on: 14/02/2016.

BELEI, Renata Aparecida; GIMENIZ-PASCHOAL, Sandra Regina; NASCIMENTO, Edinalva Neves; MATSUMOTO, Patricia Helena Vivan Ribeiro. The use of interviews, observation and videotaping in qualitative research. Cadernos de Educaçâo | FaE/PPGE/UFPel | Pelotas [30]: 187 - 199, January/June 2008.

BERNARDO, Gustavo. *Education through argument.* Rio de Janeiro: Rocco, 2000.

BOCCATO, Vera Regina Casari. Bibliographic Research Methodology in the Dental Area and the Scientific Article as a Form of Communication. Revista de Odontologia da Universidade Cidade de Sâo Paulo 2006 Sep-Dec; 18(3)265-74.

CARVALHO, M. The Teaching of Mathematics I. Federal University of Santa Catarina. 2007

COLLARES, C. A. L.; MOYSÉS, M. A. A. The transformation of pedagogical space into clinical space (the pathologization of education). Série Idéias n. 23, Sâo Paulo, FDE, pp. 25-31 , 1994. Revista Projeçâo e Docência, vol. 3, n° 2.

http://revista.faculdadeprojecao.edu.br/index.php/Projecao3/article/view/294/189. Accessed on: 05/02/2016.

CORSETTI, Berenice, et al. Professor x avaliaçãoçâo: uma reflexâo sobre sua pràxis. Cadernos da FAFIMC, Viamâo, n. 26 jan/jun/2001.

COSTA, D. K. da. *Chemistry education through research:* a path to autonomy. Porto Alegre,

2003.

DEMO, Pedro. *Great thinkers in Education:* The challenge of learning, moral formation and evaluation. 2ed. Porto Alegre: Mediaçâo, 2002.

ENRICONE, Délcia. *Teachers and innovations.* In: ERICONE, Délcia (Org.). Being a teacher. 3. Ed. Porto Alegre: EDIPUCRS, 2002.

FIGUEIREDO, N. *M.* A de. *Mètodo e Metodologia na Pesquisa Cientifica.* / 3ª Ed. Sâo Caetano do Sul, Sâo Paulo: Yedis Editora, 2008.

FUJISAWA, D. S. The use of games and play as a resource in physiotherapeutic care for children: implications for the training of physiotherapists. 2000.

Dissertation (Master's in Education) - Faculty of Philosophy and Sciences, Paulista State University, Marilia, 2000.

GATTI, Bernadete, A. *The teacher and evaluation in the classroom.* Studies in educational evaluation. Sao Paulo; Fundaçâo Carlos Chagas, n. 27, jan/jun, 2003. Available at: http://br.groups.yahoo.com/group/analisetextual2003/ Accessed on: 08 / 03 / 2016.

GRILO, Marlene. *The teacher and teaching*: the encounter with the student. In: ENRICONE, Délcia (Org.). Being a teacher. 3 ed. Porto Alegre EIPUCRS, 2002.

HOFFMANN, J. M. L. *Avaliaçâo: mito e desafio* - uma perspectiva construtivista. Ed. Porto Alegre: Mediaçâo, 2009.

HOUAISS, A; VILLAR, M. de S; FRANCO, F. M de M. *Dicionàrio da lingua portuguesa*. Rio de Janeiro: Objetiva, 2001.

JESUS, José Sérgio; SILVA, Maria das Neves. A Study of the Factors that Impact on Low School Performance. December 2012.

LUCKESI, Cipriano. Interview on learning assessment, given to Jornal do Brasil and published on July 21, 2000. Jornal do Brasil, July 21, 2003.

LOCH, J. M. P. *Avaliaçâo: uma perspectiva emancipatória. Quimica nova na escola,* Sâo Paulo, n. 12, 2000.

MARQUES, Mârio Osorio. *Writing is necessary:* the beginning of research. Ijui: Unijui, 2003.

MORAES, R. A storm of light: understanding made possible by discursive textual analysis. Ciência & Educaçâo: Bauru, SP, v. 9, n. 2, p. 191-210, 2003.

OLIVERIA, S. A. MORAES, A. G. *The register as an official alternative in the recycled schooling of the PCR:* how do teachers proceed in relation to teaching and assessing the learning of the alphabetic writing system? 2005. Text submitted to the XIII ENDIPE, 2005.

PIZZANI, Luciana; DA SILVA, Rosemary Cristina; BELLO, Suzelei Faria; HAYASHI, Maria Cristina Piumbato Innocentini. The Art of Bibliographic Research in the Search for Knowledge. Revista Digital Biblioteconomia e Ciência da Informaçâo. Campinas, v.10, n.1, p.53-66, jul./dez. 2012 - ISSN 1678-765X.

RAMOS, M. G. Educating through research is educating for argumentation. In: MORAES, R. LIMA, V. M. do R. Research in the classroom: trends for education in new times. Porto Alegre: EDIPUCRS, 2002.

SANT'ANNA, Ilza Martins. **Why evaluate? How to evaluate? Criteria and Instruments**. Petrópolis, RJ: Vozes, 1995.

SANTOS, Katia Guiomar Lesonier dos; RECK, Vanessa Costa Corrêa;

NASCIMENTO, Rosangela Conceiçâo Gomes. A Brief Look at Qualitative and Quantitative Assessment Practices in a Public School. XVI Interinstitutional Seminar on Teaching, Research and Extension. Disponivel em: http://www.unicruz.edu.br/seminario/artigos/humanas/UM%20BREVE%20OLHAR%20SOBRE%20PR%C3%81TICAS%20DE%20AVALIA%C3%87%C3%83O%20QUALITATIVA%20E%20AVALIA%C3%87%C3%83O%20QUANTITATIVA%20EM%20UMA%20ESCOLA%20P%C3%9AB.pdf. Accessed: 17/11/2015.

SANTOS, S. G. *Modalidade de avaliaçâo* (2009). Available at: www.cds.ufsc.br/~saray/Modalidades%20de%20avaliacao.pdf Accessed on: 08 / 03 / 2016.

SILVA, André Luis Silva da. Dificuldades do Educando em Quimica e Fisica, 2010. http://www.infoescola.com/pedagogia/dificuldades-do-educando-em-quimica-e- Fisica/. Accessed on: 04/01/2016.

SILVA, José Maria da; SILVEIRA, Emerson Sena da. *Presentation of academic work:* norms and techniques. Petrópolis, RJ: Vozes, 2007.

SOUSA, Georgyna Batista de Carvalho. Effectiveness of Qualitative Assessment in the Teaching-Learning Process. Article in Mundo Jovem magazine, 2010. Available at: http://www.mundojovem.com.br/artigos/a-eficacia-da-avaliacao-qualitativa-no- teaching-learning-process.

SOUSA, José Francisco de. Evaluation as a process of knowledge construction. Available at: http://www.webartigos.com/artigos/avaliacao-como- processo-de-construcao-de-conhocimento/49769/ Accessed on: 01/04/2016.

SOUZA, Tito Eugênio Santos. MENEZES, Afonso Henrique Novaes. Evaluation in Distance Education: Concepts and Possibilities. REVASF, Petrolina, PE, vol. 4, n. 6, p. 158-170, dec. 2014.

VILLAS BOAS, B. M. *Portfolio, evaluation and pedagogical work.* Campinas, SP: Papirus, 2006.

## QUESTIONNAIRE APPLIED

1- Do you know what garbage is?

( ) yes ( ) no

2- What do you do with the waste you produce?

( ) Throw it in the garbage can

( ) Separate for selective collection

( ) Throws in vacant lots or on the ground

( ) Other

3- What do you do with the waste you produce at school?

( ) Throw it in the garbage can

( ) I select and look for the selective collection garbage cans

( ) I don't bother, I play anywhere

( ) I keep it and look for a garbage can to throw it in

4- Do you know what selective collection is?

( ) Yes ( ) No

5- Would you separate your household waste for recycling in your municipality?

( ) Yes ( ) No

6- Do you know how to properly separate waste for recycling?

( ) Yes ( )No

7- Do you usually reuse any materials that go to waste? a) No, because I don't know how to reuse materials.

b) No, because garbage should be thrown away.

c) Yes, I turn shoe boxes into gift packages or use them to store other objects

d) Yes, I use pet bottles to store the oil I no longer use, or other materials.

e) Yes, I use the bags that used to go to waste to do my shopping.

8- Do you care about environmental issues?

( ) yes ( ) no

9- In your opinion, should the landfill receive all types of waste?

a) Yes, because this is what he was made for.

b) Yes, as long as you know which waste can be thrown in the landfill.

c) No, because hospital waste needs to go elsewhere.

d) No, because materials like batteries need to go back to the companies and have a different fate

10- Do you know what slurry is?

( ) yes ( ) no

11- Do you know where your municipality's waste goes?

( ) yes ( ) no

12- Do you know what recycle, reuse and repurpose mean?

( ) yes ( ) no

FSC
www.fsc.org
MIX
Papier aus verantwortungsvollen Quellen
Paper from responsible sources
FSC® C105338

Printed by Books on Demand GmbH, Norderstedt / Germany